D1177591

HOLE IN THE THE GARDEN WALL

I am
the seeker.
I will find the
hole in your garden wall
and set you
free.

The story behind this photograph represents one of the many strange phenomena which guided my efforts on this book. Originally, I envisioned a colorful rose-covered English garden wall as the title plate, but circumstances forced me to take the photograph in early spring, long before roses bloom in northeast Ohio. Five possible locations were chosen before shooting began on the Saturday before Easter Sunday, 1986. Four of them produced no image strong enough to match the verse. Driving to the fifth, I was suddenly compelled to stop at Gilmour Academy, a private boys' school I had never before seen nor visited. In a formal garden behind the Academy's Tudor mansion I found my hole in the garden wall. And something more. After the master print was developed I noticed a perfect crucifix of light centered in a crown of thorns. Others have studied the print and found as many as 12 additional hidden images. Not one of them was evident to me when photographing the wall.

HOLE IN
THE
GARDEN
WALL

PRUDENCE KOHL

Foreword by Dr. Inez C. Jeffery

**CYRANO GUILDMASTER
PUBLISHING**

1988

Library of Congress
Card Catalogue Number 87-73562

ISBN 0-945299-00-1

Book and dust jacket design by David Gibbs,
The Design Group,
Greensboro, North Carolina 27403

Printed by the Walnut Circle Press
Greensboro, North Carolina 27409

Published by Cyrano Guildmaster Publishing
P.O. Box 22151, Beachwood, Ohio 44122
First edition, 1988

My first encounter with Prudence Kohl was one of delight and challenge. Each of us had responsibilities in an international congress planned by others which was not going well but she was the essence of poise and mental assurance, positive the spin-off would be worth the effort. Indeed it was. It gave me a continuing workship and friendship with this rational, practical, creative genius.

All of Kohl's artistic and business accomplishments are special because she approaches them in unusual and convincing ways. Her personal philosophy and approach to life are totally positive. She believes in her ability to do a perfect job whether it is an unconventional approach to corporate communication or expressing her innermost thoughts in ways which will help others spin webs of hope and strengthen their own possibilities.

Dreams are held close and are very precious to most of us. Expressing them could lighten the world but the timid feel inadequate and threatened. To them, dreams may be like fairy tales in which they dare not put stock for fear they might appear too impractical. Kohl is neither threatened by her dreams nor by helping others to fulfill theirs. She is neither hesitant to tackle the most practical assignments nor to walk on rainbows, then talk and write about both as if they were daily events.

In a world fraught with so much violence and disdain, we need relief from the steady onslaught of pessimism. We often hear, with terrifying emphasis, that there is no precedence for the ills which beset us. We hear that changes and advances have been so rapid we are unprepared to deal with them. Literature, however, has endured and moved mankind for centuries. Its influence is recorded. Kohl dares to say nothing brings words closer to human experience than poetry. No other literary format delivers more pressure per word and more power per line than verse.

Kohl has chosen photographs and verse as her mode of expression. This artist has a special ability to plumb depths, sense what others think and feel, then translate those thoughts and feelings into images and words with masterful precision. It is her unique gift which exemplifies her personal philosophy to touch others that they might realize an expanded awareness of the world they live in.

According to Kohl, effectiveness in human affairs depends on our ability to reach beyond mediocrity, elevate the level of public debate over social issues and remove the prejudicial insulation which separates us from each other. Kohl's work reaffirms a belief in fundamental human rights and the dignity and potential of every human being. If we are to make a difference in creating a better world for everyone, it behooves each of us to work on our own self-image. It is the only starting point that makes any sense.

In Kohl, the rare combination of rock bottom practicality and artistic creativity comes from her ability to take life experiences, good or bad, and make them work for her and those around her. She makes rapid evaluations and solid decisions and is able to drop meaningless activity if it violates her sense of human dignity. Her innermost convictions have been garnered from testing all aspects of life. She is skilled in communicating those convictions to all who care enough to share what she so generously offers.

With her photography and poetry, Kohl points the way to a new level of thought. Whether humorous or serious, the message is always there. Through her visions and verse she makes the commonplace a link between forgotten experiences and a sudden inspiration for renewed dedication. Such awareness can trigger identity with our dormant dreams and make life meaningful and productive.

Kohl has had the satisfaction of developing her art her own way without the distraction of being taught how it should be done. Our literary geniuses did it their way and their work has survived the ages. We read the same thing over and over again when the words touch our experience and have a message for us as individuals.

An idea woman, Kohl is dedicated to resolving the difficult issues we face in a turbulent society. Her approach has always emphasized developing total human potential rather than working piecemeal through limited effort and undefined goals. She has written public policy speeches for business executives and strategic management programs for Fortune 500 corporations. She has taught public speaking courses, lectured on organizational development and initiated product-market strategies for major businesses. She has given freely of her talents and time to domestic and international organizations. Such efforts have brought her respect and recognition from public figures and private citizens around the world. She is one of the few who moves between the world of business and industry and the world of art and essence with confidence and grace.

The heart and soul of the artist have dominated Kohl's successful careers. But as a fine arts photographer and writer, she has come full circle in her aesthetic appreciation and ability. Her work has appeared in juried shows, private collections and galleries in Ohio, Maine, Massachusetts, New York, Florida, Oklahoma, Texas, California and Alaska and this is only the beginning. She has received more than thirty awards in writing and photography as she continues to share her unique interpretation of life with all its facets.

As you pick up this book, look forward to a rich experience. It is a combination of images and verses which will spark in your consciousness a heightened appreciation of the ordinary. As so often happens when the usual becomes art, we wish we had thought of it. Kohl's vision, talent, compassion and her willingness to share them all will bring many unforgettable moments to the reader.

Inez C. Jeffery
Doctor of Philosophy
Cultural Foundations of Education

ACKNOWLEDGMENTS

I simply cannot mention every individual who has played a role in helping me create this book. If I did, these acknowledgments would become as lengthy as an acceptance speech at the Academy Awards. For those people not mentioned in the pages of this diary, it is my hope I have thanked them in other ways. If not, my profuse apologies. But there are several people I must name, people whose contributions pushed this labor of love into reality.

Many thanks to Bruce Clapper and his associates at the Walnut Circle Press for daring to print an art book unlike anything done before and giving it the personal attention, insight and execution it never would have received from any other printer on the block.

Many thanks to David Gibbs for accepting the book's graphic design challenge, then delivering a refined design statement equal to the sensitivity, power and intimacy of the message within. His input, humor and patience turned something good into the best it could be.

Many thanks to my studio models, particularly the professional and patient James Weir and Mia Reneé, and the beautiful children at the First Baptist Child Care Center of Cleveland Heights, Ohio.

The gentle man who printed the color photographs has asked to remain anonymous, as he always does, though his reputation as one of the most gifted in his field makes anonymity nearly impossible. Respecting his request, I will call him the Master Magician and thank him for generosity beyond the call, extraordinary talents freely given, sensitivity rarely found and remembering the hungry years. Indeed, for everything he is and ever did for me, my deepest appreciation.

Finally, I thank my husband, Gary, for encouraging this square peg to get out of the round hole of organizational bureaucracies, then allowing me the freedom to find my own way up the mountain. I thank him for his sacrifice of staying in a business world that will never fully appreciate his exceptional gifts so the world might appreciate mine. May this book repay him in some small way for the nine-year, interest-free investment he made in my future.

To touch another with your heart and mind
To teach that person how to fly
Is the most difficult thing you will ever do
But everyone has a butterfly deep inside
Waiting to be free.

Dedicated to everyone who has heard the butterfly deep inside.

CONTENTS

OVERTURE

*"Obedient children do not
turn around in church."*

So reads the eleventh commandment
in the gospel according to Mother,
a stoic interpretation of biblical law
which made the act of peering
over the back of one's pew as sinful
as idolatry. Consequently, every
Sunday morning I sat, face forward,
staring at the posterior of Mrs.
Brindel's asinine hats, fantasizing
on what could be so horrific at the
rear of our little church that God
would smite an innocent six-year-old
for a quick peek. Was Satan residing
in the last pew waiting to incinerate
any delinquent child who broke
Mother's Law? Maybe I'd see our ven-
erable church elder, Mr. Whittaker,
nodding off during the sermon,
exposing a dastardly character flaw
only I would know and never disclose
unless of course he received an
appointment to the Supreme Court.
To quell my insatiable curiosity, I
joined the youth choir just to sit in
the choir loft which faced the entire
congregation. I discovered Lucifer
was not a member of our church,
but Mr. Whittaker did sleep through
nearly every sermon. Fortunately,
his reputation was safe. He pursued
a career in pharmaceuticals, not law.

*"Eat all your vegetables.
There are children starving
in India."*

Parents have taken considerable poetic license with this edict. Starvation moved from one exotic location to another to keep abreast of the latest headlines. But to an eight-year-old whose visions of the world extended no further than the Union Street Elementary School, kids starving in Buffalo, New York, would have elicited the same guilt. I shudder to think how many children received force-fed admissions into the Free World's Clean Plate Club. When I enthusiastically offered to send all my untouched Brussels sprouts to the kids in Bombay, Mother was not amused. As none of our family pets would stoop so low as to eat a sprout, I was left no alternative but deceit—stuffing the mealy green aliens into my mouth, feigning a cough to conceal spitting them into my napkin, then excusing myself from the table to destroy the evidence. I thought it a masterful illusion. It was years before my parents revealed they were too entertained by my antics to interrupt the performance.

"Nice girls don't wear make-up."

Even I knew this was a whitewash for a more sweeping condemnation: "Girls who wear make-up are Catholics or hussies." This might have been a desperate ploy by Mother to protract my childhood or virginity. More likely, it was the kind of moronic justification that breeds within insulated communities, like my home town, where the most visceral prejudice centered on a rivalry between Protestants and Catholics—heady stuff in the 1950s. All I knew was my dearest friend and role model, Ginger Bley, was a Catholic and she wore make-up. (At least I think she did. No one could be that pretty without some assistance.) Hussy or not, she was everything I wanted to be—prom queen, class president, senior salute leader and all-around Miss Popularity. My wishes never came true, probably because I was a Presbyterian who didn't wear make-up. Which is another way of saying I was a conscientious student, an accomplished musician, a pituitary gland waiting to explode and the class clown type-cast as the lead in our senior play. All in all, a "nice"

girl not to be mistaken for a hussy. And never mistaken for popular, a serious deficit when peer group acceptance is more important than innuendos on one's sexual conduct.

In retrospect, such true confessions are both amusing and revealing. Most of us were similarly landscaped throughout childhood, meticulously planted with the values and traditions dear to our families and cultures, then pinched, pruned and cultivated in the hopes we would grow into something better than the best qualities possessed by our gardeners. It's hard work, setting expectations for others' lives. No wonder walls are built around each garden plot to prevent cross-pollination which might contaminate the vulnerable seedlings.

Unfortunately, even Eden had its serpent. No garden is completely impervious to the world outside its walls. Life has a way of pressing in, forcing us to consider alternatives other than the black and white absolutes bred into us by our environments. As we mature, things never look quite so concrete as they did in our youth or to our parents. Each person we meet, each adventure we pursue beyond the garden wall challenges us to reevaluate our landscaping and, if necessary, transplant the flower beds to reflect our own talents and desires rather than those we've been taught to imitate. It is the difference between being what others want us to be and living the lives we were born to live. It's the difference between letting our imaginations and intellects be limited by mediocrity's preconceived notions and thinking for ourselves. In short, it's the difference between merely existing and truly living.

One way or another, most of us outgrow superficial childhood taboos. I now turn around in church anytime I please. Brussels sprouts and I have reached an understanding: I don't eat them; they don't make me feel guilty. And I learned to use make-up without converting to Catholicism. These decisions were relatively easy. None threatened the sacrosanct teachings of my youth.

But choosing to take responsibility for your own life is infinitely more difficult. Choices frequently involve personal risks. You may become a target for criticism,

rejection, even ostracism. At best, you stand alone for doing the unthinkable. At worst, you can never "go home" again. Society, omnipotent guardian of "shoulds" and "oughts," bestows no favors on those who assault the walls of racial prejudices, religious dogmas and social sanctions which separate the head from the heart and isolate individuals from their neighbors next door and around the world. There are no tangible awards for such inner effort. But there are rewards of a different kind for those who dare to seek the hole in their garden walls. I know from experience.

Machiavelli wrote, "There is nothing more difficult to take in hand, more perilous to conduct, or more uncertain in its success than to take the lead in the introduction of a new order of things." His words became my proclamation on employment as I ricocheted through seven jobs in 11 years. But nothing was more difficult, perilous, nor uncertain in its success than the day I admitted I was not master of my fate, captain of my soul. That was the day I relinquished control of my

life to the obsession within, stood still long enough to listen to the butterfly inside, then followed its path across the Rubicon. Today, my garden is richer and more beautiful for having done so. What I learned along the way is what this book is all about.

HOLE IN THE GARDEN WALL is an anthology of ideas and impressions recorded in the diary of my life, then transposed into vision and verse. It took 42 years to gather the raw material; 42 years of teacup tragedies, blind alleys, extraordinary people and enough pleasure to counter the pain endured while searching for a purpose greater than myself—one magnificent obsession worthy of my individual talents and gifts. In my diary, experiences are only stage settings for the human drama. What is more important are the things learned from having lived through the experiences. Specific events are unique to each person. But all people participate in a common emotional life, the fountainhead of a universal conscience. And emotions, feelings, knowledge and wisdom were meant to be shared. In doing so, I hope to touch others so they might realize an expanded awareness of themselves and the world outside their garden walls.

A personal diary is no place for a lengthy dissertation on photographic and journalistic techniques. However, a few brief comments may clarify the "visual thought" process. All photographs were taken with two 25-year-old Pentax 35mm cameras. I shun sophisticated, expensive equipment. To me, the art and magic of photography happen in the darkroom where the artist has the greatest latitude for creative expression.

Except for the Irish folk song and two favorite quotations—one from W.H. Auden, one from George Washington Carver—all verses are original, selected from the colorful tapestry of an oral history inherited from exceptional people who crossed my life's path and moved me with their strength, honesty and humanity. The words are written in the language of the storyteller, orchestrated for the ear not the eye. Their emotional power and musicality are best appreciated when read aloud.

I am frequently asked which comes first, image or verse? There is no pat formula. The inspiration starts with a message which becomes an obsession. If I am conscious of that message, it usually appears first in verse as it did in the "Schoolhouse" and "About Face." If the message remains subliminal, the photograph comes first as in "Winter Speaks" and "Last Mooring." On rare occasions, both happen simultaneously as they did in "Mavericks." The marriage of image to verse is anything but haphazard. No photograph can overwhelm its words; no verse can over-play its image. Together they must say something more than either could say alone.

I believe if you want people to think, first let them feel. To accomplish this, I use words and images for reasons beyond pure technique. The printed word invites attention to language. It is the most effective medium for communicating ideas and ideas are what move society, not technical wizardry. Photography invites attention to images. It is an effective medium for conveying impressions, feelings and emotions. By joining the power

of ideas to the power of emotions, I can tell a story neither words nor images alone could tell.

This book speaks to those people who want to become more than spectators in the drama of their own lives, people who want to contribute something to humanity beyond themselves. It speaks to the seekers who have the courage to doubt cherished beliefs in order to learn to think and feel for themselves. Above all, it speaks to everyone who continues to search for the hole in the garden wall.

Prudence L. Kohl

Experience follows expectation.
You cannot have tomorrow
What you will not risk today.

The
truths
you
seek
are
already
known

The
power
you
desire
you
already
own

You
shall
reap
what
you
have
sowed

For
ignorance
is
self-inflicted
wisdom
self-bestowed.

Quest

Fireweed and Fog,
Alaska

Knowledge is not a flower to be plucked

but a mountain to be climbed.

The trick to formal education is to not let it interfere with learning.

The Schoolhouse

Patience is a virtue
not easily learned by some
and never by others.

Infinity

The lesson is how not to will

They move most swiftly who stand still

You're only lost until you see

You're lost because you want to be.

W. H. Auden, 1907-1973

Through A Child's Eyes

All children are born color-blind,

blessed with the promise of perfect vision.

It is the one condition of childhood

I wish more parents would copy, not cure.

Dinkey

Definition of a business loss: the promise of genius crushed by mediocrity.

Caves

The

unknowns

become

the

cutting

edge

of

maturity.

About Face

When brevity is not the soul of wit, it is the mask of ignorance.

Nothing ignites the moral indignation of parents like a threat to the dreams they embrace for their children. This is particularly true when the threat is disguised as divine prophecy. So when Karl Marx perceived the road to hell paved with good intentions, then George Bernard Shaw envisioned a hell full of musical amateurs, I knew I was twice doomed. Fifteen years of my youth would be sacrificed in the name of one holy crusade waged by my parents to save ten little fingers and one soul from eternal damnation.

Piano lessons began at age three. So did my introduction to the Pygmalion effect which presumed if I attended enough concerts, was bombarded with enough lessons and exposed to enough musicians, I would become a pianist through osmosis. And if the final product was something less than the second coming of Rubinstein, teaching piano was a noble second career considering the alternatives—like being a public relations flak or a floozy.

For more than 10 years, the burden of this metamorphosis fell upon the shoulders of one piano teacher, Anna Kowalska Bley, alias The Miracle Worker. She was an imposing figure, an international celebrity of renowned musical virtuosity. To an easily intimidated seven-year-old, she was larger than life. I felt insignificant as a tick in her presence.

The hallmark of her teaching methods was a passion for technique. That explained why an audition was a prerequisite for becoming her pupil. I can't remember what trivial thing I played, but I played it with perfect posture and curled fingers, demonstrating everything I knew about passionate technique. Of all the recitals and competitions performed under her tutelage, none was more frightening than that first audition, probably because Mother was sitting across the room nervously clutching her purse. To fail the audition would be a minor infraction. To fail Mother's master plan for my future would be a mortal sin. Maybe Anna Bley sensed my desperation and accepted me more out of pity than promise. Whatever her reason, I felt indebted for life.

So began an extraordinary love relationship between teacher and pupil. Admittedly, it was a distant love, one built on respect and not intimacy, but love nevertheless. I was no prodigy but Anna knew how to mold potential and she created an exceptional student pianist from her labors of love. Even music critics were impressed. I practiced, performed and competed while

Mother kept a scrapbook on every recital, medal and award received. Her dreams for the two of us were unfolding exactly as she planned. Or so it seemed until that wretched age of 17 when the butterfly inside stirred for the first time.

After years of emotional regimentation and discipline to other people's expectations, I crawled out from under a rock and discovered self-expression. Music was no longer a means to an end but the most personal, powerful means of communication I had yet experienced. Music offered me an outlet for my passion undiminished by adult compromise. It was the ultimate privacy. When I spoke through the piano, absolutely no one could interfere and only those tuned to my intensity would understand the message. Pursuing a career in music would infringe upon and eventually destroy my new-found inner sanctum. So I rebelled. My last act of defiance came moments before what would be my last public performance.

It happened at my high school commencement. I had the dubious honor of performing a piano solo during the program. At the appointed time, I found myself standing in the stage wings waiting for some dignitary to finish his rhetorical drivel so I could begin Brahms. Peering out at the faces in the audience, I concluded no one, except my parents, was interested in hearing Brahms. Why waste passion on those who don't care? These folks had come to witness a milestone in human evolution —closing the door on adolescence; opening the gate to maturity. They had come to see both a conclusion and a beginning. The least I could do would be to give them half what they expected —a conclusion. I vowed I would never compete nor perform in public again. To this day, I have never broken that vow.

For the last 25 years, I've played the piano for the sheer passion and pleasure of it. What I lost in technique I gained in emotional sensitivity. The piano now speaks the language of my feelings as it never could in the hands of a teenager. For me, virtuosity is not measured on the concert stage but in the sanctuary of my home, in those private moments between me and my studio grand. It's not important thousands of people hear what I say. To know I can say it is enough. And for that, I sincerely thank my parents and The Miracle Worker.

At age seven
it took me six
weeks to hammer
"The Happy Farmer"
into a state of seige.
My battle-weary teacher
immortalized both the struggle and the page
with one of those fancy gold stars. At the
time I thought it an honorable tribute to my
tenacity. Now I know, the honor really
belonged to Anna Kowalska Bley.
For if music is the voice
of angels, surely no
teacher ever marched
so far into hell for
such a heavenly
cause.

The Impossible Dream

Interlude

You can play a tune of sorts on the white keys,

You can play a tune of sorts on the black keys,

But for real harmony, you need both the black and white.

George Washington Carver, 1864-1943

Sometimes the only thing separating inspiration from stagnation is a man-made wall.

Deep Lock

You are as dead now
as you choose to be.

Stumps

You were born the stuff of legends, a Contender to the Game,
Every movement calculated to bring honor to your name;
City fathers had you cast in bronze and seated on the Square
Had your laurels boldly chiseled in the stone beneath your chair.
And there you sit, your visage a vantage point for birds
If silent lips could speak the truth, then surely these the words:
"Time erased my memory, my glory quickly passed,
Fame is but illusion, it's the pigeon poop that lasts!"

EPITAPH

Band Man

Some people take life too seriously

and play not seriously enough.

One can approach the study of American history as a tedious recital of chronological events or as a peep show featuring the human foibles of ordinary people who, because of time and circumstance, found themselves face to face with destiny. I prefer the second option, studious voyeurism. It makes me more tolerant of my country's immaturity, its arrogant myth of exceptionalism and three indelible stains on its conscience—one for the annihilation of the American Indian tribes, one for the Civil War holocaust, and one for the vilification of the Vietnam veteran.

I will never learn all I should about our native Americans, but I know all I want to know about the Civil War and Vietnam from one day spent on a battlefield called Gettysburg.

My husband and I visited the Gettysburg National Military Park for the first time in October, 1981. Arriving at the Visitor Center, we received an orientation on troop movements and military strategies which locked Union and Confederate soldiers in the bloodiest battle of the Civil War. We then plotted our own tour of the park and for the next five hours walked where thousands of men had walked and died during three catastrophic days in July, 1863.

At no time did either of us feel a blush of pride at what we were seeing. Because what we saw was a sanitized vision of war, the kind of laundered synopsis we used to read about in our high school textbooks. We knew we stood on soil once soaked with so much human blood the waters of Plum Run ran sticky red. In contrast to manicured grounds and impressive statues, we envisioned what President Lincoln saw when he arrived at Gettysburg, four days after the carnage, to dedicate a small section of the battlefield. The gut-wrenching stench from thousands of mutilated bodies and putrified horse carcasses had to be more than 15,000 genteel visitors could stomach. Lincoln promised "the dead shall not have died in vain." He assumed Americans would forget his words but not the horrible consequences of war. Instead, we immortalized his address and forgot why it was delivered.

Two thousand markers and monuments to the dead brought us no rush of patriotism, just a profound repulsion at so flagrant an exhibition of human error and waste. It was incomprehensible. We wondered what General George Pickett said to his troops that could rally 12,000 foot soldiers, many of them teen-age boys, to march shoulder-to-shoulder across an open field to certain slaughter. To be sure, war is hell, the basest of Man's neolithic instincts raised to a deadly power. But more heinous than war is the inflammatory rhetoric which justifies, then sanctifies such acts of human degradation.

Every hour spent at Gettysburg opened wounds from Vietnam. The parallels were frightening. One century after the Battle of Gettysburg, my husband was fighting a hopeless war in Southeast Asia—with teen-age soldiers. He fought it, others opposed it, most of us succumbed to a national amnesia fostered by a continuous media blitzkrieg of both the serious and sensational. In time, the two became indistinguishable and we, the audience, indifferent. That is the dark secret of war — everyone becomes a victim one way or another.

For my husband, Vietnam was a war of personal conflict between duty and conscience, morality and mortality. He was raised to love one's country, serve it and die for it if need be. The reality that one might have to kill others in the process was lost in the moral righteousness of embellished patriotism. Was it any different, this personal conflict, for the soldier at Gettysburg? Could he justify killing his brother as a worthy sacrifice for preserving the Union or the Confederacy? Did a 16-year-old boy love life so little because he loved his country so much? Or was he duped by banners and military bands? I wish I could have put my ear to the ground at Gettysburg and heard an answer.

Damn those who sow the seeds of war from their arm chairs and lecterns. Damn those who dare to editorialize from the sanctity of their dens and offices. From Gettysburg to Vietnam and every war in-between, it is the soldier who pays

the price for the world's zealots. The Vietnam soldier not only paid the price, he bore the brunt of his country's humiliation and shame.

I did nothing with the photographs taken at Gettysburg. I was lucky to have any at all. It's hard to focus with tears in your eyes. There was one image of a woman, cannon and trees silhouetted against a sunset which was particularly appealing, but no image alone could express what I felt that day on the battlefield. So all photographs went into a box, out-of-sight, out-of-mind.

It took four years, a granite wall and LeRoy Martin to add the missing pieces to what eventually became "Voice From A Gettysburg Grave." LeRoy was a friend and Vietnam veteran who spent Memorial Day, 1985, at the Wall in Washington, D.C. When he returned, he shared with me the personal catharsis he experienced touching those etched panels bearing the names of familiar and unknown comrades who did not

return from Southeast Asia. He spoke of the stranger who took his arm and said, "Welcome home, soldier." He had waited ten years to hear those words. At last, his sacrifice was acknowledged.

Deeply moved, I went home and retrieved the photograph of the woman, cannon, trees and sunset, placed it next to my typewriter and waited. The words finally came from somewhere inside my soul like water over a spillway. Only five words were changed in the original inspiration.

When the "Hole in the Garden Wall" photo and verse collection is exhibited, "Voice From A Gettysburg Grave" carries this special notation: *inspired by and dedicated to the Vietnam veteran*. It is also dedicated to a new kind of American patriot, those men and women who can rise above the prejudice of closed minds in search of an inner strength for themselves and their country which cannot be easily nor fatally insulted. Because of people like that, tomorrow's heroes may never have to pay so dear a price for their patriotism as did the heroes at Gettysburg and Vietnam.

VOICE FROM A GETTYSBURG GRAVE

Bend ear to earth,
  you who walk this killing field,
  and I will tell the truth about
  what happened here.
I was 15 when a Rebel cannon
  put me in my grave.
Me and 51,000 others.
All dead in three days.
More than a century has passed
  and still you haven't learned
  the terrible legacy left behind
  in this savage place.
Learn it now
  and I will not have died in vain.

War is a grotesque deception,
  born of Man's prejudice,
  fed by a nation's wounded pride,
  inspired by the rhetoric of
  self-righteous indignation.
Of these three,
  rhetoric is the most destructive.
From twisted delusions spring words
  which rise to omnipotence,
  wreak havoc on humanity,
  then vanish suddenly in the light
  of a thousand bloody mornings after.
Words rallied my soul
  but could not bring it back from the dead.

So speak no eulogies for me.
Words will never cleanse my blood
  from this soil.
Nor the blood of your fathers and sons
  from the soil of
  Compiegne, Bataan,
  Anzio, Korea, or
  Vietnam.
Witness this mass grave called Gettysburg
  and remember this:
Words kill.
The first victim is truth;
  the second, reason;
  and the third, human life.

BOOTHBAY SUMMER

Last Act of Autumn

Real change happens only from the inside out,

never the other way around. Appearances

are little more than external statements

of an internal condition.

Winter speaks eloquently in shattering silence.

Winter Speaks

If one small seed can breach a wall of stone,

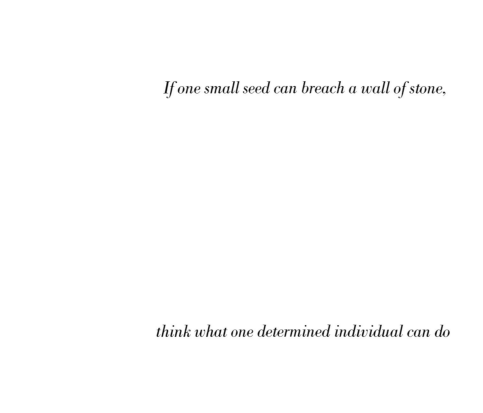

think what one determined individual can do

against a world of indifference.

Perseverance

Stonewall

Somewhere between the rocks and a rule book, we set our own limitations.

Bell and Cross, Santa Fe

Any

institution

which

makes

its

walls

more

important

than

its

soul

is

doomed

by

its

own

egotism.

A MIRACLE OR TWO

It's a blessing to know in a world too
commercialized
compromised
computerized
demoralized
hypnotized
jeopardized
plagerized
scandalized
scrutinized
synthesized
and
traumatized
there's still room for a miracle or two.

THE MIRACULOUS STAIRCASE

In 1852, the Sisters of Loretto left Kentucky for La Villa Real de la Santa Fe de San Francisco de Assisi. In this Royal City of the Holy Faith they founded the Loretto Academy of Our Lady of Light. Some 21 years later, Mexican carpenters began construction of the Academy's Gothic chapel using architectural drawings patterned on the Sainte-Chapelle in Paris. When the structure was nearly finished, an unfortunate error became obvious—no provision had been made for access from the sanctuary floor to the choir loft at the rear of the chapel. All who were consulted for solutions to this problem agreed—a staircase was impossible; there was not enough room.

As an act of faith, the Sisters of Loretto made a novena to St. Joseph. On the last day of that novena, a bearded man whose physical characteristics were neither Indian nor Mexican stopped at the Academy, his only possessions a donkey and tool chest. The Mother Superior granted him permission to try to do what had defeated the efforts of five other master carpenters.

His masterpiece of construction was built with only a saw, T square and hammer. The circular staircase has 33 steps which make two complete revolutions, 360 degrees each, with no center support. It rests against the choir loft at the top and the chapel floor at the bottom where its entire weight appears to be supported. The wood in the curved stringers is spliced in seven places on the inside, nine on the outside, each forming a perfect curve. Wooden pegs instead of nails were used throughout. Architects and engineers from all over the world have come to ponder this "impossible" feat of construction, claiming the staircase should have collapsed with the first footstep. Yet it still stands after more than a century of continual use. Only the banister has been added for safety reasons.

The sawmill which supplied lumber for the chapel construction has no record of any wood being purchased for this project. In fact, the wood is a hard-fir variety, nonexistent in New Mexico. Where it came from remains a mystery to this day. And when Mother Magdelene attempted to pay the carpenter for his labor, he was nowhere to be found.

Adobe

Footprints in Dust

Will

the last

human be

as the first,

a cave dweller,

holed up in the

shadows of a mind

that swept the ceiling of

the cosmos and sifted

sands from the seven seas,

but remained ignorant to

the end of Man's

true purpose

here

on Earth.

Even a desert blooms in its own time.

Desert Blooms

Mavericks

Mavericks who do not
color within the
lines will never
be confined

by the pompous
proper boundaries
set by less
courageous minds.

I dream of a place without crowds, no pulsating throngs of people to shatter my spirit nor shorten my stride.

I dream of a place where mist makes love to mountain, of serrated peaks caressed only by the wind, where I can stand on rock and behold the threshold of heaven.

I dream of a place where I can walk free with the wolf and deer, witness the miracles of birth and death, and feel again the harmony of Nature's grand design.

I dream of a place where white waters plunge into mountain pools and the leviathan is neither threatened nor challenged in its dominion over the deep.

I dream of a place where land and humanity are equals, where solitary wilderness will never know the crush of Man's heel nor be plundered in the name of commercial zeal.

There is such a place. Its name is Alaska. But if you have never seen this foreign country masquerading as a United State, it may be too late. For discovery has put her on a collision course with the best intentions of Man's worst trivial pursuits.

Alaska is a carnivorous land, compressing time into a singular dimension, swallowing up extremes of scale like a gigantic black hole. Geographically, she boasts 33,904 miles of shoreline, three million lakes large enough to mention, half the world's glaciers, 365,000 miles of rivers and 19 peaks higher than 14,000 feet. Her entire population numbers approximately 420,000, fewer people than live in Cleveland, Ohio.

She has been called a carnival side show of every gargantuan and infinitesimal manifestation on the North American continent. Indeed, P.T. Barnum would have been impressed by her invincible mountains juxtapositioned with an arctic tundra so fragile it can be scarred forever by a single footprint.

Alaska's secrets hide within her duality. But the romantic fantasy of the last frontier springs from her outrageous size which fuels a uniquely American chauvinism. From the past to the present, pioneers have approached her challenges with a swaggering bravado. The game was to best nature, to conquer the land or at least bend it to fit some intellectual persuasion. As if scaling Mount McKinley, striking gold, finding oil, or protecting the caribou was its own aphrodisiac that promised to eradicate a life of personal impotence.

Will we ever learn to read what history has faithfully recorded? Romancing a fantasy exists only as long as the search. The dream dies upon discovery. All that remains is the residue of trying. And Alaska bears more than her share of scars from those who tried to force their wills upon her land.

I would hate to think we are doomed to repeat history because we refuse to heed the handwriting on the wall. It would be folly to minimize Alaska's importance to Mankind by prolonging the tedious filibuster between those who see her significance only as a bonanza of natural resources and those who advocate preserving her wilderness from encroachment by any human being. Perhaps one day soon a great compromiser will rise above the ash can of zealots and pronounce Alaska to be what she really is— the last great experiment, a final dress rehearsal for us to prove we have learned something from our past mistakes and choose not to repeat them for future generations. If so, Alaska will never again be called the last frontier, but the first in a new chapter on human compromise and survival here on Earth.

Keystone Canyon, Alaska

Alaska is not the last frontier, but our last chance to prove ourselves worthy of so great a natural inheritance.

Muscle and Steel, Cleveland Flats

Bridge to Nowhere

If what is essential is invisible to the eye
why does Man continue building
temples and towers?
Wisdom holds that all facades will be laid bare
upon the sands of Time—
as surely as the sea will pillage
the ghostly remains.

KITTY HAWK PIER

A person comes of age twice in America. The first rite of passage is from adolescence to adulthood, heralded by promises of what is to come. The second is from employment to retirement, haunted by what was or could have been. It is difficult to accept Robert Browning's gentle invitation, "Grow old along with me! The best is yet to be…" in a society that worships youth and physical beauty with a maniacal vengeance. Probably no subject more accurately mirrors America's peculiar blend of social and religious dogmas than the prospect of growing old. For too many, aging is a one-way ticket out of the mainstream of the living and useful. A rational dialogue on death and dying is still taboo in large sections of our society.

Instead, we gild the wolf in sheep's clothing with superfluous labels to mask our apprehensions—what we hope old age will be, not what it really is or could be. We call retirement the "golden years" and retirees "golden-agers." The ubiquitous symbol for retirement is the gold watch, an especially perverse graven image to industry, and now the lack of it, presented by the world of business.

Propelled by such symbolism, the pendulum swings between two extreme stereotypes of the elderly. One suggests a Norman Rockwell painting—life imitating art. Aged parents are embraced by the family, children and grandchildren attend to their every whim, all live in harmony and dignity under one roof until the ancient ones pass along. At the opposite extreme stands the nursing home, ghastly monument to senility, loneliness and shame. Here guilt-ridden families come incognito to dispose of their elderly like so much excess baggage.

According to government statistics, neither stereotype represents the majority of our older citizens. But statistics don't reveal the magnitude of the human issue at stake. I need no numbers to illustrate the trauma experienced by one man who suddenly found himself a passive spectator in the drama of his own life. No figures can measure the impact on this man's self-esteem when his employer put a ceiling on his productivity, equating age to obsolescence. I witnessed the second coming of age when my father-in-law retired in 1972.

For 46 years, he worked as a nameless number in a large conglomerate's personnel file. He occupied a bookkeeper's cage where he maintained fastidious ledgers in longhand. Within his sphere of influence, the introduction of an electric adding machine was a technological revolution. He needed no golden handcuffs to keep him in his chair. He was the very model of the Puritan work ethic, born and raised with the idea if a company condescended to hire you, you owed it your loyalty and life. To have a job was a privilege. During the Depression, it was a luxury. He assumed full responsibility for his family's financial security. Money earned was never used for personal pleasures. It was earmarked for posterity as tangible evidence of parental love. Neither serious illness nor broken bones kept him from his work. During more than four decades of employment, he missed fewer than 10 days on the job.

He was granted a two-year extension beyond mandatory retirement because his services were needed to bring the accounting department into the computer age. Forced to retire at 67, he was removed from his primary source of identity and self-worth. There were no pre-retirement planning seminars to assist in the transition.

As his title was not "important" enough to warrant a gold watch and testimonial send-off, several of his colleagues treated him to dinner. That was that. He came home intoxicated and spent the night crying on the bathroom floor.

He is now 83 years old, a simple man with tastes and expectations to match. His understanding of world events does not extend beyond the boundaries of his hearth and neighborhood. The morning newspaper is gospel; the eleven o'clock news, the absolute truth. Home is his ultimate security where one's usefulness is as tangible as a job

list. In all, he is an exemplary citizen. He also is not poor enough to qualify for most of the programs for the aged his taxes helped support, not rich enough to protect his money from the tax man.

His life offers only one observation on growing old in America. But even one life can speak a truth and his emanates from somewhere in the gray area between "The Hands of Jack" and "Matron of the Marketplace."

Photographing the old woman was a bittersweet experience in eaves-dropping. Walking down an alley behind the outdoor produce

stalls at Cleveland's West Side Market, I heard an old woman arguing with the younger attendants in a fruit and vegetable stand. Her words were both strident and desperate, resurrecting a painful twinge of deja vu inside of me. I stood riveted in place, gawking from behind a pyramid of discarded crates. Pointing his finger, an agitated young man told the woman to get out of his way, to stop interfering with business. She retreated to an upturned basket. I raised my camera and waited. Several minutes passed before she straightened her back, put hands to knees and turned her head in my direction. Her face was such an unforgettable portrait of resolve and defeat, I felt the need to apologize for invading her private thoughts. Instead, I pressed the shutter. I never saw her again. I don't even know her name. But because of one photograph and the words it inspired, she will never be forgotten.

Maybe it was Jack's agelessness that impressed me, or maybe that infectious twinkle in his eye, something of a cross between Santa Claus and a leprechaun. I just knew I felt young in his presence, especially when he told those enchanting stories about his life as an artist. Here was an older man with an unquenchable thirst for learning and artistic expression. He had earned the right to apply and perfect his talents however he chose and he chose a road that rises above prescribed cultural roles and social expectations. His mind and spirit showed no deterioration. Like rare books, they had precious secrets to share with anyone wise enough to hear the spoken summary of one man's personal heritage.

In a world which too often favors credentials over character and titles over talent, his was a message for all ages. Wisdom is indeed the legacy of one's life. The older person has every reason to share it with others. The young have every reason to listen and learn. This is the ultimate act of communication which will lead to an understanding among all generations. And this is the message of "The Last Mooring."

HANDS OF JACK

Matron of the marketplace
memory of a distant race lost
amid the garbage and the flowers
portrait of a brutal truth
society prefers its youth
the golden myth cannot redeem
a spirit broken by the dream
no one hears your urgent plea
remember me
remember me

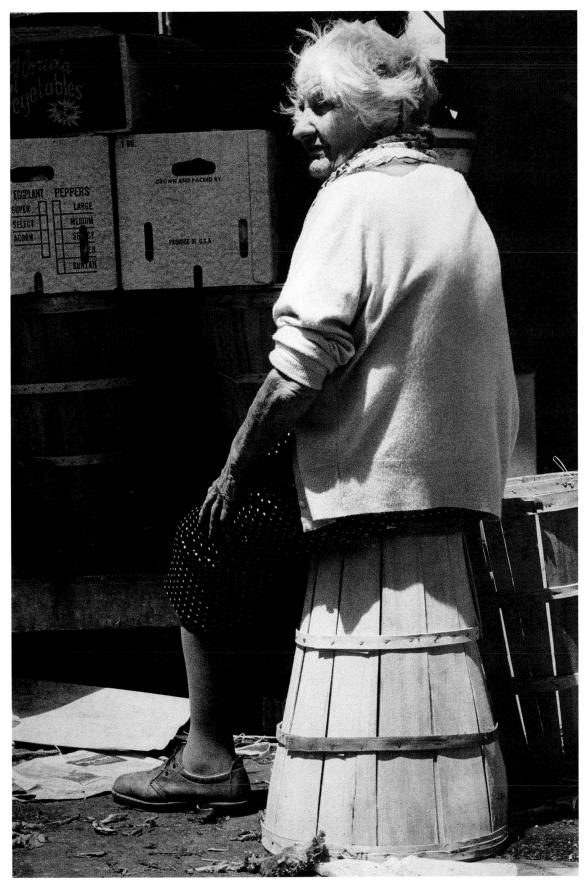

Matron of the Marketplace

Last Mooring

Age exacts its own initiation dues.
Yet there is something heroic in those persons
and things who refuse to surrender in the face of time.
To them belongs a dignity denied the young and foolish
who chase the wind.
Look into the still waters around each aged frame
and see yourself in the reflection of that which was
but has yet to be.

FIRE AND ICE

At sixteen, I learned to kiss with my mouth open, many thanks to Marty Head and a secluded picnic table at Chestnut Ridge Park. Just over the threshold of seventeen, I experienced my first torrid infatuation, many thanks to Jim Smith, whose only negative attribute was his junior class status. But when you are a senior and no beauty queen, you seek your Casanovas anywhere you can find them. And he was a prize worth the ridicule of crossing class lines.

At one of those teen-age tribal dances following a basketball game, Smitty gave me his class ring. Not even the residual stink from a sweaty gymnasium could diminish the rapture of that moment. My euphoria and his ring lasted one week. The poor lad simply buckled under the pressure of his incredulous peers who questioned why one so high in the popularity polls would be seen in public with one so indistinguishable as I. Two weeks later I attended the homecoming dance unescorted, disguised as the school mascot — a bulldog. Considering the recent assault to my self-esteem and puppy love gone amok, it seemed the only proper thing to wear. Such is love at a fragile seventeen.

At eighteen, I met a cultured man who introduced me to cerebral love. He was a professor, I his dream weaver who wrote poetry and played Chopin as he said it should be played. He was erudite yet worldly-wise, a man of cultivated tastes who treated me with the same awe and respect he gave to his vintage Rothschilds and rare antiques. I was his treasure, placed on a pedestal, under glass, to be admired from afar. It was a gallant gesture wasted on one feverishly impatient for an intimacy his plutonic relationship would not permit. Admiration was not enough for a woman-child who had just discovered hormones two years earlier. What's more, there is precious little air under a bell jar and no place to move on a pedestal but off. So I left in search of a less elevated place in someone's heart, sadder but wiser for the lessons learned from a patient older man.

In the summer of '64, I found fire and ice in one young man. I met my Jekyll and Hyde in the Wyoming mountains where we spent three months redefining ecstacy. At least I did. He was six-feet, 200-chiseled-pounds of smoldering white heat. To a naive girl yet deceived by images, he was a gift from the gods. Dr. Jekyll told me the woman he marries would be treated like a queen. I must have been distracted by the scenery. I didn't hear the part about his role as absolute monarch.

Blinded by his fire and sword, I changed my mind, my priorities, my very life without even asking where we were going. I left college, friends and family in California to be near him in the East, not knowing what I would do once I arrived on his stoop. I was consumed by a passion which placed him at the center of my sanity. For nearly four years, I was the only paying passenger on his roller coaster of hysterical idiosyncracies. Four months from our wedding day, Mr. Hyde beat me into a sobering reality. Fire turned to ice under the weight of his brutal fists. My innocence died that night in a West Virginia motel room along with my belief in the power of physical appearances.

It seems a thousand years have passed between those days of bulldog disguises and finally understanding a higher love than I ever thought possible in a world gone mad with instant gratification. Remembering the words of Robert Frost, I took the road less traveled by and that made all the difference. He spoke the truth. So do I...

There is a higher love
    beyond your physical desires
    above your sensual dreams
Seed of one's destiny
    it is fired by creativity
    and cooled in the light of divine purpose.
To fuse with another human being
    is the highest form of spirituality
    you will ever know
But approach with caution and respect—
    fire is rarely gentle
    and ice can burn as deeply as the flame.

Illusions in Black and White

The world is a comedy for those who think,
a tragedy for those who feel.

I met my love in the days of the spring,

Summer he gave me a gold wedding ring,

Autumn he built me a house made of stone,

Winter he left me to live there alone.

I'll bank the fires with the black bogs of peat,

Love's full of waiting and love's bittersweet,

Spring is coming and brooks they will sing,

I'll still be wearing my gold wedding ring.

Irish Folk Song

Desertion

To be alone is a matter of choice;

To be lonely is a matter of circumstance.

One is a conscious decision;

The other, a cry for help.

Alone/Lonely

Fowl Moon

Teaching someone to French kiss can be so tedious.

It's amazing how a little sex can change your POINT OF VIEW

Some men go blind staring into darkness;
some from staring into the light.

Blind Stairs

How sad to know two people can spend a lifetime searching for each other and never touch. Sadder still when two people do find each other, read life's meaning in each other's eyes, but won't dare breach the walls which separate the two from one. So it is for many lovers who knock at the garden gate, only to be denied access. So it was for me, once upon a time.

When one who follows the heart loves one who serves the mind, fear and misunderstanding are the fatal consequences. The margin for human error is devastating. Love disintegrates into a game of priorities and pride. A thousand apologies cannot repair the shattered dream. Perhaps the heart can express its desires more openly than the mind permits. Or perhaps the mind needs only itself to be complete, but when it comes to fulfilling the heart, it takes two.

Twenty years ago, a young cavalier taught me well the price paid when the wizard cannot escape the tyranny of his own logic—when reason gets in the way of truth. I wrote the lesson on the twenty-second page of my youth and called it Farewell Oz.

FAREWELL OZ

We played at love
    behind the garden gate
    charades in a world of make-believe
But I was vulnerable
    and chivalry is dead.

You enchanted me with red balloons
    and I, seduced by a dozen strings,
    hung on.
Your fables lifted me above the wall
    where I could see eternity
    but not blood beneath the rose.

Too soon the sun set
    the hour came
    for you to put away your toys
Speak to me of men and boys
    beyond the daffodils and dreams.

The man-child never said a word
    deceit was the only sound I heard
Your fairy tale came true;
From you, I learned the art
    of breaking hearts.

My Lochinvar of a thousand lies
    what games you played
    for the fatal prize
    and always by your rules.
I played your game of love and lost
But I was vulnerable
    and chivalry is dead.

Good-bye yellow brick road.

Freedom only comes from bondage.

Freedom

Joshua Rocks

The search for self-worth begins
by finding what is indestructable within,
then letting it be.

No place so safe as in my father's arms.

Father & Son

There is no wall, no fence, no barrier
Enough love cannot tear down.
No matter how hopeless the outlook,
    how muddled the tangle
    how great the mistake
The power of love will conquer all.

Barn & Vine

Corn Crib

TO MICHAEL, WHEREVER HE MIGHT BE

It was not serendipity that made the loon and lighthouse synonymous to Maine. You have to be a bit loony to live there year-round and a bit loony to leave for any reason. I know. I'm one of those summer fair-weather fowls who returns to the rocks of Pemaquid Point with seasonal regularity, broods for a time beneath the Portland Head Light, then heads south, too fragile a species for Down East winters. Still, every departure leaves a tiny hole in my heart.

But for those born with the map of Maine in their genetic codes, leaving is nearly impossible, rather like denying one's birthright. Should any native-born son or daughter foolishly attempt an out-of-state sabbatical, consider it a temporary lapse in sanity. Mother Maine is very patient. She provides hundreds of lighthouses to guide her prodigal children home. I know because I knew Michael.

Michael was born in Bangor, entered the priesthood, earned his bachelor's degree in theology, served God as personal consultant to the Bishop of the Portland Diocese, received a masters in psychology, left the priesthood, married, became director of psychiatric and social services for 750 inmates at the Cleveland Corrections Center, then went home to raise sheep on a 100-acre farm in Greene, Maine. A summary of his career qualifications would begin with "an innate ability to find effective solutions through experiential problem-solving," and end with "a man of great integrity." But where, in the vernacular of business resumes, can one describe the humanity of this exceptional man? Where does one explain the pain, the struggles that shaped the character of a man who changed the lives of nearly everyone he met? For me, that change followed these five words: "Do something with your photography." Because I listened, I will never be quite the same again.

What more can one say about a man whose personal philosophy became his legacy, a man who said, "I dedicate my life to those too gentle to live among wolves." That he was beautiful, sensitive, vulnerable, a man out-of-step with the times? He was all these things and a great deal more. Michael was one of those rare individuals who left permanent footprints behind though he walked gently on this earth.

Michael liked people regardless of form or function. And people stuck to Michael like burrs to a squirrel. House rules included serving meals to any number of strangers any hour of the day or night. He was a gifted listener who never breached a single confidence. With or without the requisite priest's collar, he would hear a confession anytime, anywhere. Like a Maine lighthouse, Michael cast his light into the storm so others might find their way. They usually did.

He crossed the Rubicon to self-reliance not once, but three times.

He left the brotherhood for lack of closure. The day he turned his back on religious hypocrisy was the day he abandoned an easy God of canonized ritual. He left the organizational bureaucracy for lack of commitment. The day he turned his back on political subterfuge was the day he abandoned the hierarchical world of vanity and false promises. The day he opened his photo gallery in Boothbay Harbor was the first day others could see his unique vision of the world through a talent too long denied. That his entrepreneurial endeavors never materialized into all they could be was the price paid for impatience, not inadequacy. For whatever private reason, Michael could not choose between what his head told him to do and what his heart inspired him to be.

Michael was more an illusionist than a photographer. Through his eyes, the simple and mundane became exquisite. He used camera and film to translate his extraordinary visions and feelings into something more permanent. Such beauty from a man who was nearly blind but not too blind to compose his own final vision.

Like so many men landscaped by a Catholic childhood, Michael possessed a psychic black hole, an insidious inner sanctum to his personality only he was allowed to enter. It was a place of punishment where feelings of inadequacy and intimidation crescendoed into ultimate self-condemnation. From the bowels of this terrible hole came an unshakable belief he would die at age 53, succumbing to a kind of Gothic curse which already had taken five other family members. No intellectual, emotional, nor spiritual persuasion could penetrate the wall surrounding his fatal vision.

A haunting loneliness began to separate the two of us. Yet I never stopped loving Michael for all the pain of trying. In the end, I could not touch his spirit as he had touched my soul. Maybe a man can choose his time of death. Maybe he already knows it at birth. I do know Michael moved to a subconscious rhythm only he understood and when that rhythm changed, he crossed the Rubicon for the last time. He died in September, 1985, at age 53.

It is appropriate the remaining photographs and verses in this book be dedicated to Michael who made all this possible. Each is a tribute to life, love and friendship. They address the attraction of Maine, the indecision to leave Ohio, the dark side of the 53 prophecy. They capture his transformation, immortality and legacy. And the final photograph, selected from Michael's own private collection, speaks of his universality as does the message he sent through me to all humanity.

Head Light

Driftwood

Beware the paralysis of analysis.
The decision to make no decision is the worst decision of all.
More enterprises have been shipwrecked by paralyzed imaginations
than by taking
calculated
risks.

Communicating with the living is only slightly more difficult than communicating with the dead.

Tombstone

Finale

At the twilight of mortal dreams,

one soul stands on the warp

between heaven and earth,

sees a Light no mortal sees

and passes into eternity

through the window of a sunset.

Like the rocks and the sea, the human spirit lives forever.

Spirit Gate

I dedicate my life to those
too gentle to live among wolves.

MESSAGE FROM MICHAEL

Come, fill your sails with the breath of life.
Keep your appointment with the universe.
Choose a course equal to that challenge
and you will never
be the same again.
Let no man set your boundaries.
Let no wall block your view.
Love all you see and do.
And when you hear the butterfly deep inside
let it go
set it free
set it free.

Mast

My "visual thought" approach to communication has always been the wellspring of all my artistic efforts, as unique to my writing and photography as the technical methods used in creating images and verses.

Each photograph is a master print. Every negative is developed by hand using light as a painter uses oils. Only one master print is made from each development process. In the Hole in the Garden Wall exhibition collection, most of the verses are written in my own hand, then matted and framed as an integral part of the finished piece. Because prints and handwriting can never be exactly duplicated, each finished piece is uniquely different.

Although it took 42 years of living and learning to compose the verses in this book, only the last nine years were devoted to photography. I first used a 35mm camera in August, 1978. Two months later, I received my first major commission, though at the time I didn't know the difference between an f-stop and a shutter speed.

In 1984, I studied the principles of black and white photography under the tutelage of Bruce Cline and Richard Walker. In April, 1985, I had my first public one-woman show exhibiting 33 photographs. Three months later, more than half the collection had been put to verse. During that time, I was haunted by five words— "hole in the garden wall." It was not until January, 1986, I realized those words were the title of a book, a visual diary composed of lessons learned from my life experiences.

So, although it took 42 years to find this one magnificent obsession, it was only during the last 20 months I was aware that seemingly unrelated thoughts, verses and photographs from years past would eventually be galvanized into one unified creative endeavor entitled, *Hole in the Garden Wall.*

The following program notes provide more specific details on where and when each photograph was taken and, if needed, some additional insight on what inspired me to create a particular verse or visual composition. Such information is included only to pacify those with insatiable curiosities about who, what, when, where and why. It is my hope people will interpret the greater messages in their own way. Because when it comes to interpretation, there are no such absolutes as the five W's.

The lead verse into the body of the book is exceptionally powerful. It needed an equally powerful visual illusion. Three separate photo efforts ended in failure, each one too anemic compared to the verse. Just before my deadline, desperation forced me to print a negative I had not previously considered. The print showed something I didn't see in the proof sheet— the profile of a face gazing into light. This human element and the subliminal illusions created by the clouds added the missing elements which energized the verse. So it is no exaggeration to say this visual image was literally pulled out of the clouds.

This is the oldest photograph in the collection, taken from the first roll of film I ever shot with my Pentax Spotmatic. I was told, by no less a reliable source than a native Alaskan, the fireweed is the state's natural barometer. As blossoms die down the main stalk, winter approaches. Of course, I also heard the legend the other way around—winter approaches as blossoms fall off bottom to top. So much for the accuracy of local folklore. I did not wait for an Alaskan winter to find out which version of this tale was true.

My personal thanks to the Geauga County Historical Society for granting me permission to photograph the interior of this beautifully restored schoolhouse at Burton's Century Village. May this image forever be a reminder of a simple truth: formal education may be confined by the rules and regimentation of bureaucratic structures, but true learning can never be confined by its physical limitations.

I have no idea where this was taken—somewhere near a Union Soldiers' Cemetery in Ohio's heartland. It isn't often I take such obvious liberties with a photo, but in this case, the verse justified exercising some poetic license. Upside-down, an otherwise pleasant image assumed a new identity and vitality by forcing a viewer to rethink perspectives, testing one's patience to adopt different spacial relationships. Those too impatient for anything less than absolute realism (probably the same folks who peek at the answers to crossword puzzles) can have it their way by turning the book upside-down.

When this photo entered its first competition, it was titled, "Seagulls in Silhouette." It didn't win, perhaps because the judges couldn't find the objects in the title! The verse is the conclusion of W.H. Auden's "Labyrinth," a message which profoundly influenced my life for many years. But it took five years for image and verse to find each other.

For two years, I struggled to finalize a mental image to match the power of this verse. Using only one child was too limiting, too trite. But to find several children of different racial or ethnic backgrounds all in the same place whose parents would allow them to be photographed seemed an impossible task worthy of a small miracle. Fortunately, I believe in miracles. I met these four beautiful children at the First Baptist Child Care Center in Cleveland Heights, Ohio. They are, from top clockwise, Carmen Licate, Qing Quan, Catherine Young and Jaryn Slaby. After weeks of securing the necessary clearances and releases, I had exactly one chance, 20 minutes, to recreate what I saw in my mind's eye. This is the one photograph in the collection twice blessed by miracles.

Thinking of a creative, sensitive former colleague who once confided to me, "I always thought if I kept my nose to the grindstone, played by the rules and exceeded my job expectations, I would rise in this organization," no sadder words could be said about mediocrity's effect on individual aspirations. How frustrating it is to know every organization has at least one person who could have reached the stars and saved the dinosaurs, except for feet trapped in the tar pit of bureaucratic inertia. There is no financial loss greater than the loss created by stifling one employee's desires and dreams.

This is one of three photographs taken during an

extraordinary afternoon at one of the few Indian cliff dwellings where visitors are allowed to roam free at their own risk. And the risk is considerable when one is alone, shouldering a full complement of camera equipment and climbing from one level to another on hand-hewn tree ladders as ancient as the dwellings themselves. It took me five hours to scale the mountain. "Caves" was photographed at the first level and matched to a verse I've held dear to my heart since age 16. "Footprints in Dust" was taken midway up the mountain from inside one of the cave homes. Its verse was written 10 months later. "Mavericks" was photographed at the top of the cliff dwellings and both image and verse happened simultaneously which is rare indeed. I stood on sacred ground and remember feeling a peculiar surge of inspiration, as if the Ancient Ones had something important to say and were using me as their conduit. I was completely alone, yet not alone at all.

page 22
ABOUT FACE   1987
MODEL: JAMES WEIR

Shakespeare's Polonius deserved to be skewered through a wall tapestry. He spoke only a half-truth about brevity. Anyone sensitive to human relationships knows there is a dark side to the soul of wit which obliterates the line of distinction between wit and a wag.

page 29
INTERLUDE   1984

I read the biography of George Washington Carver at age 15. He was an exceptional visionary who spoke many quiet truths. But these four lines moved me the most and touched my life long before the civil rights movement pricked our national conscience in the 1960s. The words made sense to me then. They make even more sense today and tomorrow.

page 30
DEEP LOCK   1986
OHIO CANAL LOCK #28
CUYAHOGA VALLEY NATIONAL
RECREATIONAL AREA
PENINSULA, OHIO

In many ways, the Cuyahoga River Valley in Northeast Ohio is like a great lady. Age has given her dignity. An extraordinary past has brought her national attention and prestige. Indians, missionaries and pioneers left footprints in her soil. She outlived them all. Not so the Ohio Canal. A century of neglect and dry rot has eaten away most of the canal banks and wooden lock gates. What few locks remain stand in silent testimony to a time in the mid-1800s when a flourishing canal trade brought a young Ohio recognition as a major contributor to the nation's marketplace and made it the third most populated state in the Union. The canal program was to provide a vital link between the eastern seaboard and the western territories—an all-water route from New York to Cincinnati called the Ohio-Erie Canal. But the great canals which helped build the interior of a young United States were abandoned in the name of progress. Horse-drawn boats proved no match for the iron horse.

page 32
STUMPS   1982
PRATT ISLAND, MAINE

This swampy area at the side of an unmarked dirt road was reminiscent of a stage setting from the Star Wars Trilogy, home of Yoda, classroom for Jedi knights. The verse seems worthy of Yoda's wisdom,

something he would share with those old enough to understand its many implications. For in decay, there is always the promise of growth, as in death there is always the promise of life. Where we find ourselves in the cycle of life is where we choose to be.

page 35
EPITAPH   1985
STATUE OF TOM JOHNSON
PUBLIC SQUARE
CLEVELAND, OHIO

page 36
BAND MAN   1985
CHARDON, OHIO

He was the brass man in the Rube Band which entertained visitors to Chardon's annual spring Maple Syrup Festival. The photograph was spontaneous and unposed, though I was very fortunate he turned his head toward the camera the moment I pressed the shutter. It is one of my favorite portraits, perhaps because he reminds me of a character from a Charles Dickens' novel. Or perhaps because he has such an appealing expression on his face. I have tried unsuccessfully to locate this gentleman. I hope we meet again some day so I might thank him for all the pleasure this portrait has brought to me and many others.

page 49
PERSEVERANCE   1984
PRATT ISLAND, MAINE

This was the first photograph put to verse in 1985. In retrospect, I find it fascinating that the words "stone" and "wall" appear in this verse as if both were a subconscious prediction of a theme and book title yet to come. Many of the photo compositions taken before 1986 included walls, fences, gardens and stones, as if someone or something knew about this book long before I did.

---

page 52

BELL & CROSS   1986
SANTA FE, NEW MEXICO

Design and color were the inspirations for this photograph. The composition was simple, clean and uncluttered, the expanse of adobe broken only by the oblique line of the bell rope. This old adobe church near Santa Fe is a study in contrasts to the new adobe structures being built in Old Santa Fe, like the Loretto Inn, subject of the photograph appropriately titled, "Adobe."

---

page 63

DESERT BLOOMS   1986
JOSHUA TREE NATIONAL MONUMENT
CALIFORNIA

---

page 68

KEYSTONE CANYON   1978
ALASKA

How this photograph came to be is proof that truth is stranger than fiction. One of the most difficult and dangerous stages in the construction of the 800-mile-long Trans-Alaska Pipeline was the section near the Keystone Canyon, a gaping, foreboding gash in the earth east of Valdez, Alaska. In honor of this herculean construction feat, one of the new super tankers, commissioned by Sohio to carry Alaskan oil, was named Keystone Canyon. The wife of one of Sohio's senior executives was selected to christen the ship. As part of this ceremony's protocol, she wanted to present the captain with a photograph of the ship's namesake, rather than a painting which was the usual gift.

Previous attempts by professional photographers met with her disapproval, for all photographed the canyon from the air during summer. She wanted a photo from the canyon floor capturing the desolate atmosphere of that lonely place. After reviewing my photos taken two months earlier during my first visit to Alaska, I was commissioned to return and shoot the Keystone. She didn't know she was betting on a dark horse, someone who knew little more about a 35mm camera than how to change film.

A bush pilot flew me into Valdez after two futile attempts to penetrate a fog bank that blanketed Prince William Sound. Once in Valdez, I couldn't get out for five days. Such are the weather conditions in mid-October. Every day I drove the same rented Pinto to the canyon and spent eight hours attempting to photograph my subject through a veil of sleet and snow with temperatures near 30 degrees and the wind chill in single digits. I'd get out of the car, crawl around the river bed until I couldn't see, get back into the car, wipe off the camera, lens, my glasses and face, wait for my clothes to dry, then repeat the whole procedure in search of another angle or perspective. Only two cars passed me the five days I was in the canyon.

In the presence of such awesome beauty, I learned a new respect for the power of nature. I also learned new definitions for isolation and human insignificance. These feelings spawned the verse which was matched to the photograph seven years after it was presented to the captain of the Keystone Canyon.

---

page 70

MUSCLE & STEEL   1985
THE FLATS
CLEVELAND, OHIO

This and "Bridge to Nowhere" are two photographs of the same railroad bridge which once carried trains across the Cuyahoga River. No longer used, it now stands permanently frozen in a vertical position.

---

page 73

OZYMANDIAS   1981
CAPE HATTERAS NATIONAL SEASHORE
CAPE HATTERAS, NORTH CAROLINA

Bracing myself against 50-mile-per-hour winds, I gazed down this isolated stretch of beach and thought only of Shelley's poem:

"My name is Ozymandias, king of kings: Look on my works, ye Mighty, and despair!" Nothing beside remains, Round the decay Of that colossal wreck, boundless and bare The lone and level sands stretch far away.

In 1985, I wrote my own verse for this image, but kept the "Ozymandias" title in honor of my original inspiration.

---

page 75

KITTY HAWK PIER   1981
KITTY HAWK, NORTH CAROLINA

It takes so much to make a memory and very little to shatter one. So I chose to keep the memories and look to this photograph to remember childhood pleasures long past in a town and city which long ago lost their innocence. Those were the summers we used to play tag around the pilings under the great pier in Atlantic City. And those were the summers we'd scavenge for coins in the damp, cool sand under Wildwood's boardwalk. Standing under the Kitty Hawk Pier, those memories were as vibrant as the real events 35 years ago.

There has always been something very tragic yet heroic, even human, about this deserted house closed for the season or maybe forever. From the first day I saw it, in the chilling winds of October, it seemed the perfect visual incarnation of an old folk song my uncle used to sing to me. As a child, the words told a story. As an adult, they speak a truth to everyone who has found themselves in any human relationship which suddenly closed for the season, or forever.

This was the hardest image to find for its verse. For more than two years, I tried to focus on what I wanted and the more I tried, the more the image eluded me. One day on an unplanned drive around Ocean Point, I suddenly saw this image. The first few compositions did not include the boat. Only after test prints were made from all the negatives did I understand that the overall power of this piece would be diluted without the rowboat in the lower right hand corner.

Just for the records, this is a Canadian goose, not a duck!

Though not planned nor intentional, many people have called this photograph the most erotic in the collection. I carry this observation one step further. Ancient alchemists viewed the physical world as four elements—air, earth, fire and water. All four elements are represented in this image if you translate fire as male and water as female, according to meta-physical interpretations. Then the photograph communicates the universal harmony and balance among all elements.

This sunset was taken just hours after Michael told me "do something with your photography." It was the last time I saw him. The verse was written in June, 1985. Michael died three months later.
I shall always wonder if he was telling me something more than I chose to consciously acknowledge that last night at Linekin Bay. If so, the verse was indeed prophetic.